Philippians

God's Guide to Joy

RON KLUG

FISHERMAN
BIBLE STUDYGUIDES

Philippians

PUBLISHED BY WATERBROOK PRESS

12265 Oracle Boulevard, Suite 200

Colorado Springs, Colorado 80921

10 Digit ISBN 0-87788-680-6

13 Digit ISBN 978-0-87788-680-8

Published in the United States by WaterBrook Multnomah, an imprint of The Doubleday Publishing Group, a division of Random House Inc., New York.

SHAW BOOKS and its aspen leaf colophon are registered trademarks of Random House Inc.

Printed in the United States of America

2008

10 9 8 7 6 5 4 3

Contents

.

How to Use This Studyguide

*F*isherman studyguides are based on the inductive approach to Bible study. Inductive study is discovery study; we discover what the Bible says as we ask questions about its content and search for answers. This is quite different from the process in which a teacher *tells* a group *about* the Bible—what it means and what to do about it. In inductive study, God speaks directly to each of us through his Word.

A group functions best when a leader keeps the discussion on target, but the leader is neither the teacher nor the "answer person." A leader's responsibility is to *ask*—not *tell.* The answers come from the text itself as group members examine, discuss, and think together about the passage.

There are four kinds of questions in each study. The first is an *approach question.* Asked and answered before the Bible passage is read, this question breaks the ice and helps you start thinking about the topic of the Bible study. It begins to reveal where thoughts and feelings need to be transformed by Scripture.

Some of the earlier questions in each study are *observation questions*—who, what, where, when, and how—designed to help you learn some basic facts about the passage of Scripture.

Once you know what the Bible says, you need to ask, *What does it mean?* These *interpretation questions* help you discover the writer's basic message.

Next come *application questions,* which ask, *What does it mean to me?* They challenge you to live out the Scripture's life-transforming message.

Fisherman studyguides provide spaces between questions for jotting down responses as well as any related questions you would like to raise in the group. Each group member should have a copy of the studyguide and may take a turn in leading the group.

A group should use any accurate, modern translation of the Bible such as the *New International Version,* the *New American Standard Bible,* the *New Living Translation,* the *New Revised Standard Version,* the *New Jerusalem Bible,* or the *Good News Bible.* (Other translations or paraphrases of the Bible may be referred to when additional help is needed.) Bible commentaries should not be brought to a Bible study because they tend to dampen discussion and keep people from thinking for themselves.

SUGGESTIONS FOR GROUP LEADERS

1. Thoroughly read and study the Bible passage before the meeting. Get a firm grasp on its themes and begin applying its teachings for yourself. Pray that the Holy Spirit will "guide you into all truth" (John 16:13) so that your leadership will guide others.

2. If any of the studyguide's questions seem ambiguous or unnatural to you, rephrase them, feeling free to add others that seem necessary to bring out the meaning of a verse.

3. Begin (and end) the study promptly. Start by asking someone to pray that every participant will both understand the passage and be open to its transforming power. Remember, the Holy Spirit is the teacher, not you!

4. Ask for volunteers to read the passages aloud.

5. As you ask the studyguide's questions in sequence, encourage everyone to participate in the discussion. If some are silent, try gently suggesting, "Let's have an answer from someone who hasn't spoken up yet."

6. If a question comes up that you can't answer, don't be afraid to admit that you're baffled. Assign the topic as a research project for someone to report on next week, or say, "I'll do some studying and let you know what I find out."

7. Keep the discussion moving, but be sure it stays focused. Though a certain number of tangents are inevitable, you'll want to quickly bring the discussion back to the topic at hand. Also, learn to pace the discussion so that you finish the lesson in the time allotted.

8. Don't be afraid of silences; some questions take time to answer, and some people need time to gather courage to speak. If silence persists, rephrase your question, but resist the temptation to answer it yourself.

9. If someone comes up with an answer that is clearly illogical or unbiblical, ask for further clarification: "What verse suggests that to you?"

10. Discourage overuse of cross references. Learn all you can from the passage at hand, while selectively incorporating a few important references suggested in the studyguide.

11. Some questions are marked with a ✍. This indicates that further information is available in the Leader's Notes at the back of the guide.

12. For more information on getting a new Bible study group started and keeping it functioning effectively, read *You Can Start a Bible Study Group* by Gladys M. Hunt and *Pilgrims in Progress: Growing Through Groups* by Jim and Carol Plueddemann. (Both books are available from Shaw Books.)

SUGGESTIONS FOR GROUP MEMBERS

1. Learn and apply the following ground rules for effective Bible study. (If new members join the group later, review these guidelines with the whole group.)

2. Remember that your goal is to learn all you can *from the Bible passage being studied.* Let it speak for itself without using Bible commentaries or other Bible passages. There is more than enough in each assigned passage to keep your group productively occupied for one session. Sticking to the passage saves the group from insecurity ("I don't have the right reference books—or the time to read anything else.") and confusion ("Where did *that* come from? I thought we were studying _____.").

3. Avoid the temptation to bring up those fascinating tangents that don't really grow out of the passage you are discussing. If the topic is of common interest, you can bring it up later in informal conversation after the study. Meanwhile, help one another stick to the subject.

4. Encourage one another to participate. People remember best what they discover and verbalize for

themselves. Some people are naturally shy, while others may be afraid of making a mistake. If your discussion is free and friendly and you show real interest in what other group members think and feel, the quieter ones will be more likely to speak up. Remember, the more people involved in a discussion, the richer it will be.

5. Guard yourself from answering too many questions or talking too much. Give others a chance to share their ideas. If you are one who participates easily, discipline yourself by counting to ten before you open your mouth.

6. Make personal, honest applications and commit yourself to letting God's Word change you.

Introduction

*O*ne of the most joyful books ever written came from a man in prison who was facing possible execution. The man was Paul, and the book, his letter to the Philippians. It has been called the "epistle of joy" because it reverberates with the words *joy, glad,* and *rejoice.* The theme of the book is "I rejoice; you can rejoice too."

All who are seeking more joy in life—and that means nearly everyone—can find in this short book God's guide to joy, written by a man who faced head-on all the evils and troubles of the world—misunderstanding, sickness, abandonment by friends, persecution by enemies, imprisonment, doubts, despair—and yet could say, "Rejoice in the Lord always. I will say it again: Rejoice!" (Philippians 4:4).

With the help of this studyguide, you will approach Paul's letter to the Philippians *inductively;* that is, instead of being taught someone else's conclusions about the book, you will be led to discover its truths for yourself. This is important because it is often the truths we discover for ourselves that stay with us to influence and shape us.

The questions in this studyguide will help you discover for yourself the situation in which Paul was writing, the problems facing the Philippians, and Paul's inspired message to them. Other questions will help you apply Paul's message to your own life.

While our attention will be on the letter to the Philippians, we will look from time to time at other parts of the Bible that cast light on this book—especially the book of Acts, which recounts Paul's life and the experiences that led him to write this letter. By comparing different parts of the Bible, we will use a basic principle of interpretation: We let Scripture interpret Scripture.

So plunge into the study of this great letter. Let your discoveries of Paul's character and his encouragement of the Philippian church lead your spirit toward deeper commitment to Christ. And let the Holy Spirit guide you further along the path of joy.

PAUL AND THE PHILIPPIANS

PHILIPPIANS 1:1-2; ACTS 16:6-40

*R*emember the last time you sat down to write a letter to a good friend? It probably began with a resounding "hello," and the words that followed were likely filled with plenty of warmth and good memories. Perhaps you wondered how your friend and his or her family was faring, and you wished them well in their latest ventures. "Send my regards to the folks," you might have said, "and tell them I miss you all!"

This letter from Paul to the Philippians was written with that kind of familiarity and heartfelt longing to see old friends. Paul's salutation tells us of his confidence in and consideration for those in the church at Philippi. He sent them not only his greetings but grace and peace. And when we come to realize all that Paul and these friends had shared, we can understand why.

1. Who from your past would you like to see or talk with again? What would you say to him or her?

READ PHILIPPIANS 1:1-2.

🖋 2. Who sent this letter? What was the relationship of the letter writers to one another? What title did they give themselves?

3. What verb motivates the actions of a servant? Describe the mind-set a good servant should have.

🖋 4. To whom was the letter addressed? What are some common definitions of the word *saint?* Which one applies here?

5. In his letters, Paul used the phrases "in Christ Jesus," "in Christ," and "in the Lord" dozens of

times. What do these phrases mean to you? Why
might they have been so important to Paul?

READ ACTS 16:6-40.

6. This passage describes the beginning of Paul's relationship with the Philippians. What motivated Paul
to travel to Philippi? How did he make his first con-
tact with people there?

7. Who was the first convert? Why do you think this
was significant?

8. Why do you think Paul was troubled by the slave
girl's speaking out in such a way (verses 17-18)?

Why did Paul's action get him and his companions into such trouble?

9. What did Paul and Silas do in prison? How did God take care of them in this situation, and what was the result?

10. After reading this passage, what generalizations would you make about the church at Philippi?

✎ 11. Going back to Philippians 1:2, what two great blessings did Paul and Timothy wish for the Christians at Philippi? What does each of these words mean to you?

12. According to Paul, what is the source of these blessings? What does each of the names *Father, Lord, Jesus,* and *Christ* tell us about God?

FOCUS ON JOY

13. What does the word *joy* mean to you?

14. What clues do these passages give you about lives that are characterized by joy? How can you follow their example?

PAUL'S PRAYER OF THANKSGIVING

PHILIPPIANS 1:3-11

*J*n John Bunyan's classic, *Pilgrim's Progress,* Christian and Hopeful enter a place called Enchanted Ground on the way to the Celestial City. Hopeful becomes drowsy and begs to suspend their journey just long enough to take a nap. Christian dissuades him, "lest sleeping, we never wake more," and Hopeful learns to be thankful for such a steadfast friend. He expects that Christian will be rewarded for his faithfulness one day. The two pilgrims walk on, encouraging and assisting each other.

How often we need to thank God for the allies he sends us on our journey! In this study we'll discover Paul's thankfulness for his Philippian friends. They had been a great support to him, just as he had been for them, and he delighted in that mutual relationship. He prayed for their spiritual development—for their love, their discernment, and their productivity. Like Christian's friend Hopeful, Paul felt these faithful companions deserved a rich reward.

1. When you talk to God about your friends, what do you say?

READ PHILIPPIANS 1:3-11.

2. For what did Paul thank God? Which words in verses 3 and 4 show how strongly he felt about this?

3. What confidence did Paul have regarding the Philippians? What do you think he meant by "the day of Christ Jesus" (verse 6)?

4. If you claim the promise of verse 6 for yourself, what confidence can you have?

5. What difference would it make if you were continually aware of this reason for confidence? How would it affect your posture, your facial expression, your actions, and your attitudes toward others?

6. Which expressions in verses 7 and 8 show the close relationship between Paul and the Christians at Philippi? With what leader does your church or study group have such a close affiliation, and how can you better support him or her?

7. Identify at least four requests Paul made for the Philippians in verses 9-11. What is the "fruit of righteousness," and how does this come to us through Christ?

8. According to verse 11, what was the ultimate purpose in the Philippians' spiritual growth?

9. Think back on your prayers for people in the last two weeks. Which elements of Paul's prayer for the

Philippians were present in your prayers? For whose spiritual growth are you particularly concerned?

10. Using verses 9-11 as a model, write a prayer for yourself or for someone else. Try to express it honestly in your own words.

FOCUS ON JOY

11. According to verses 3-6, what caused Paul to feel joy?

12. Think of the people in your life who are sources of joy for you. They may be physically present or far away, as the Philippians were to Paul. List their names below. Following the example of Paul, thank God for each of these people and pray for their continued growth in him.

IMPRISONMENT FOR CHRIST

PHILIPPIANS 1:12-26

*O*nce upon a time an emperor of a far-off land heard the enchanting song of a nightingale. The emperor sent his servants to find her so that he might listen to her lovely melody whenever he wished. But when he had finally captured the bird, she would not sing. Assuming the bird was sick, the emperor freed her. The nightingale flew to a nearby tree and began to sing sweetly again.

Most of us would respond in the same way as that nightingale if we were imprisoned. What would there be to sing about if we were locked up, away from all that was important to us? As we observe Paul's response to his imprisonment, we will learn how God works through all circumstances, and how Paul always found something to sing about.

1. What would be the most difficult thing for you to endure if you were incarcerated?

READ PHILIPPIANS 1:12-26.

⚓ 2. What was Paul's attitude toward being in prison? In what two ways did his imprisonment contribute to the advancement of the gospel?

3. Why might Paul's imprisonment have made some of the other Christians bolder in speaking about their faith in Christ?

4. Do you find it easy to "speak the word of God… fearlessly" (verse 14)? Why or why not? What could help you be a more courageous witness for Christ?

⚓ 5. What two groups of people were active in preaching Christ while Paul was in prison, and what was the motivation of each?

What does Paul's attitude suggest about how we should view the work of Christian churches or organizations that are different from our own?

6. Although there was the possibility that Paul's forth-coming trial could have ended in his death, what confidence did he express in verse 19, and what contributed to this confidence? How might Christ have been honored by Paul's life and his death?

7. Explain the internal conflict Paul expressed in verses 21-24. How did he expect the dilemma to be resolved, and why?

8. Paul said, "For to me, to live is Christ" (verse 21), stating the central commitment of his life. At this

point in your life, how would you honestly complete the statement, "For to me, to live is…"? Describe some changes that would have to take place for you to truthfully say, "For to me, to live is Christ."

9. Paul expected to visit the Philippians again. What did he hope would be the results of this visit? How does this amplify his statement "For to me, to live is Christ"?

10. Review verses 12-26 and list at least six ways in which Paul mentioned the central importance that Christ had for him.

FOCUS ON JOY

11. According to verse 18, what caused Paul to rejoice? What would it take for you to develop more joy for the same reason?

12. In verses 19-20 what was Paul's hope for future joy? Upon what did this hope depend?

13. What word or concept is linked to joy in verse 25? What are some ways in which your progress in the faith—and therefore your joy—could be increased?

UNITY AND OBEDIENCE

PHILIPPIANS 1:27–2:11

*T*he dictionary defines *community* as "similarity or identity; a group or class having common interests." Our individualistic society resists the idea of common identity and interests. "I wanna be me," we say. Though we may reject the jargon, we all long for the unity and security that underlies true community.

Paul had learned from experience what would bring unity and joy to the Christians in Philippi and everywhere. "Stand firm in one spirit," he wrote (1:27). "Look not only to your own interests, but also to the interests of others" (2:4). Our attitude, Paul said, should be like Christ's. As we follow Christ's example and obey his words, we become a joyful community before God.

1. When you were younger, to what in-group or community were you eager to belong? Why?

READ PHILIPPIANS 1:27-30.

2. After Paul expressed his hope of seeing the Philippians again, what concern for them did he indicate? Verse 27 reminds us of one major characteristic of a life worthy of the gospel. How did Paul describe this?

3. What second characteristic of the Christian life did Paul mention in verse 28? How might the boldness of the Christians have been a sign to their enemies?

4. What double privilege did Paul mention for Christians in verse 29? Why would suffering be a privilege?

5. Have you ever suffered for Christ? If so, describe the reason for your suffering. What was your attitude toward it?

READ PHILIPPIANS 2:1-4.

6. What four motives did Paul give for Christian unity (verse 1)? What does each mean to you?

7. In view of these motives, what did Paul ask the Philippians to do? How did he describe Christian unity in verse 2, and how does this compare with 1:27?

8. Verses 3 and 4 describe a mind-set that would promote unity in a group. How would you apply Paul's message to your study group, church, or some other organization to which you belong?

READ PHILIPPIANS 2:5-11.

9. According to these verses, how did Jesus demonstrate the attitude described in verses 3 and 4? What was the ultimate test of Jesus's humility?

✑ 10. What is the significance of the word *therefore* in verse 9? What is the special name God has bestowed on Jesus, and when do you think verses 10 and 11 will be fulfilled?

11. "Jesus Christ is Lord" was an early Christian creed or simple confession used in connection with baptism. What actions or attitudes in your life proclaim this same confession?

Focus on Joy

12. In chapter 1 Paul stated that one source of his joy
     was the fellowship of the Philippians. In chapter 2
     he said their unity would make his joy complete.
     Explain this connection between unity and joy.
     How can discord be an enemy of joy?

13. Looking at your family, your church, your school, or
     your place of work, what could you do to increase
     the unity—and thereby the joy—that is present?

THE CHRISTIAN LIFE
IN ACTION

PHILIPPIANS 2:12-30

*T*he Christian life is not just saying a creed; it is living out what we believe. Yet often our actions and attitudes betray how little we really do believe. How much will we allow Christ's lordship to affect our everyday circumstances? How far will we go in following his example?

Paul took his Christian life to the ultimate limit: He was willing to die so that Christ would be glorified. In this passage he mentioned his friends Timothy and Epaphroditus, who were also willing to radically live out the gospel message. Paul exhorted the Philippians, and all who claim to follow Christ, to continue to obey Christ and shine like stars in a world darkened by sin.

1. What challenges have you found in your Christian life that you might never have had if you were not following Christ?

Read Philippians 2:12-18.

2. What was Paul asking the Philippians to do? What does it mean to "work out your salvation," and why must this be done "with fear and trembling" (verse 12)?

3. What is the relationship between God's working and our working? What examples can you give from your own life?

4. What characteristics of the Christian life did Paul identify in verses 14 and 15? Who do you know that is like this, and how does he or she seem to rub off on people?

5. In what ways is ours a "crooked and depraved gener-
    ation" (verse 15)? How can we shine like stars in this
    kind of world?

6. What picture did Paul use to show his willingness to
    die for Christ? How does this picture further
    enhance the idea of unity?

READ PHILIPPIANS 2:19-30.

7. What beautiful commendations did Paul give Timo-
    thy? How was Timothy an example of the kind of
    Christian life Paul had been describing in this letter?

8. What disappointment did Paul voice in verse 21?
    How have you seen this in your own experience,
    and what can you do to help your church or the
    church at large to be more like Timothy?

⌁9. Whom was Paul sending immediately, probably bearing this letter to the Philippians (verse 25)? In what ways had he ministered to Paul? What had happened to him in the process?

10. How did Paul want the Philippians to receive Epaphroditus? What does this say about how we should receive Christian workers among us?

Focus on Joy

11. In verses 17 and 18, with what words did Paul express his own joy? How did he encourage the Philippians to respond in joy?

12. Describe how this situation would prompt joy "in spite of." How can Christians rejoice in the midst of bad circumstances? If you have ever had an experience of joy in the middle of difficult circumstances, share it with the group.

THE TRUE RIGHTEOUSNESS

PHILIPPIANS 3:1-16

Sometimes we get so caught up in all the things we're doing that we forget to pay attention to who we are. Our attempts to follow the rules, get the right education, or nitpick about doctrinal issues can wear us out and often replace a living faith in Christ.

After challenging the Philippians to live in a godly manner, Paul reminded them that following rules and regulations is not true righteousness. He encouraged them to follow his example and press on to know Christ. Righteousness, Paul said, is not a do-it-yourself project. Rather, it's what God gives us through Christ.

1. What are some of your dreams or goals? How do these shape who you are?

READ PHILIPPIANS 3:1-11.

2. To what theme did Paul return in verse 1? Why did he want to repeat some things he had told the Philippians before?

3. In contrast to the insistence of some Jews on the external rite of circumcision, who did Paul say were the truly circumcised? What are the three identifying marks of the truly circumcised, the true people of God?

4. When Paul looked back on his own life, what reasons for misplaced confidence did he identify?

5. After he came to know Christ Jesus as his Lord, how did Paul reevaluate his list of "gains"? If you were to make a similar list of your religious achievements that might be the basis for false confidence, what would it look like?

6. What things do you find you must give up to gain Christ? How can our own righteousness end up being a detriment to faith in Christ?

7. In verse 9 Paul contrasted two kinds of righteousness, two ways of being in right relationship with God. What are the characteristics of each?

8. According to verse 10, what are the results of having righteousness that depends on faith? What does verse 10 mean to you?

READ PHILIPPIANS 3:12-16.

9. What major point about the Christian life did Paul make next? What metaphor or picture did he use to show the great effort required in the Christian life? In what ways have you experienced this in your own journey with Christ?

10. When Paul spoke of "forgetting what is behind" (verse 13), what kinds of actions might he have had in mind? After warning against Jewish legalism in verses 1-3, what opposite error about the Christian life was Paul warning against here?

FOCUS ON JOY

11. Paul began this chapter with the words, "Rejoice in the Lord." What do these words mean to you? How is rejoicing in the Lord different from other kinds of rejoicing?

12. E. Stanley Jones, missionary to India, wrote in his autobiography, "I'm a happy man because my happiness is not dependent on happenings, but upon the joy of belonging to him, whatever happens. That is invincible joy." How does your own experience compare with this? How can you grow in this area?

CITIZENS OF HEAVEN

PHILIPPIANS 3:17–4:3

*J*f others were to imitate your Christian life, what would happen? Knowing our own weaknesses, it's a sobering question. And not too many of us would invite people to strive to be like us.

Paul, on the other hand, unashamedly bid the Philippians to follow his example of life and faith so that they would not be led astray by foolish or evil people. Paul's instructions on how to be heavenly minded are applicable for all of us today. We, too, can put into practice his resolute trust and joyous self-sacrifice. Serving God and his kingdom prevails as our goal, for, in reality, we are citizens of heaven.

1. Name a Christian who has served as an example or model for you. In what ways has this person helped your faith?

READ PHILIPPIANS 3:17-21.

2. What right did Paul have to give such a bold command to the Christians reading his letter (verse 17)?

3. List five characteristics of the people Paul warned against. What kind of people would fit this description today?

4. According to Paul, how is the Christian different from those whose minds are set on earthly things? What can we do to set our minds on heaven while still being responsible on earth?

5. Verse 20 says, "Our citizenship is in heaven." What does this mean for modern-day Christians? What

have you learned from Paul's letter so far that will help you be a true citizen of the kingdom of God?

6. When Paul contemplated heaven as our true home, he eagerly thought of the last resurrection. What did he expect to happen? How does this compare with your own understanding of what happens after death?

READ PHILIPPIANS 4:1-3.

7. Which words show Paul's great love for the Philippians, and what, then, did he encourage them to do?

8. How might the words in verse 1 apply to the situation between Euodia and Syntyche? What would it mean for them to agree "in the Lord"?

9. Why do you suppose Paul bothered to comment on such a personal level? If you were the true yoke-

fellow Paul addressed here, how would you try to
help these women?

10. How did Paul commend these quarreling women?
    What does this suggest about the role of women in
    the church at Philippi?

FOCUS ON JOY

11. In Philippians 3:17-21, Paul referred to the resurrec-
    tion of the body and our home in heaven. Why is
    this confidence an important ingredient of our
    Christian joy?

12. In chapter 4 Paul called his Philippian brothers and
    sisters his "joy and crown." How can other Chris-
    tians evoke this kind of joy in us? How can standing
    firm in the Lord and agreeing in the Lord
    strengthen this kind of joy in his kingdom?

REJOICE IN THE LORD ALWAYS

PHILIPPIANS 4:4-23

*M*urphy's Law states that "if anything can go wrong, it will." We often groan whenever we hear this adage because we've discovered how true it can be. In contrast, "Paul's Law" might be expressed another way: "If anything can go wrong, *rejoice*." He'd even go to a greater extreme: "If anything *does* go wrong, rejoice!"

Paul said we should rejoice in the Lord all the time. The key, of course, is the phrase *in the Lord,* for only because of God's grace to us can we continually rejoice. We've seen in the book of Philippians that Paul rejoiced unceasingly. He had learned the peace and contentment of God. As we close this study of Paul's letter, let us take note of his Christlike disposition, for we have just as much reason to rejoice in the Lord.

1. When do you find it easy to rejoice? In what circumstances do you find it hard to rejoice?

READ PHILIPPIANS 4:4-9.

2. Verse 4 has been called the keynote of this letter.
   How did Paul emphasize this central thought
   throughout the book? What kind of rejoicing was
   he talking about?

∂ 3. What does gentleness have to do with rejoicing?
   What motive for acting with gentleness is given?

4. Ours has been called "The Age of Anxiety." What
   was Paul's solution to the problem of anxiety? What
   steps can you take to put this into practice?

∂ 5. What did Paul teach here about prayer? How do
   petition and thanksgiving work into the prayer
   equation?

6. What will the results of our prayer be? Why do our hearts and minds need guarding?

⚲ 7. What kinds of thoughts are to occupy our minds? Why is the quality of our thinking so important?

8. In addition to thinking correctly, what else is necessary, according to Paul? What will be the outcome of such thoughts and actions?

Read Philippians 4:10-23.

9. What had Paul learned by experience, and what seemed to be his approach toward this issue (verses 10-13)?

⚲ 10. How had the Philippians helped Paul in the past, and what was his twofold response to their help?

What can we learn about our church or our personal finances from Paul's words?

11. What two great promises could you memorize from this section? Copy them here and repeat them to yourself throughout the week.

✑ 12. Who might have been included in those who sent their greetings with Paul (verses 21-22)? How does Paul's final blessing to the Philippians encourage you?

FOCUS ON JOY

13. What is the relationship between prayer and joy? between our thinking and joy? between thanksgiving and joy? Relate a time when you have experienced joy in one of these ways.

14. In verse 4 Paul encourages us to rejoice always. How is this possible? What keeps you from rejoicing in the Lord? How can you change this?

As you close this study of Philippians, pray that God will guide you in developing a grateful and joyful heart. Then share Paul's blessing with one another: "The grace of the Lord Jesus Christ be with your spirit" (verse 23).

Leader's Notes

Study 1: Paul and the Philippians

Question 2. Paul had met Timothy when Timothy was young; the apostle became a mentor to the young man. See Acts 16:1-3, 1 Corinthians 4:17, and 1 Timothy 1:2.

Question 4. In the New Testament, *saint* simply means "a believer; one set apart for God." The bishops and deacons are the church leaders and assistants.

Question 7. Lydia originally came from Thyatira, an Asian region known for its outstanding commerce. Since the selling of purple dye was a common business in Thyatira, Lydia apparently brought her trade to Philippi because dealings would be better. "This woman was a Gentile who had accepted the highest elements in Judaism. As a woman of means, Lydia had a family and servants, who followed her example in professing faith and being baptized" (Charles F. Pfeiffer and Everett F. Harrison, eds., *The Wycliffe Bible Commentary,* Chicago: Moody, 1962, p. 1154). Although Jewish women were given some authority in the household, the women of Greco-Roman culture were given more prominence in the community than Jewish women. God used this advantage in Lydia's life to expand Christian influence in Philippi.

Question 11. It may be helpful to look up the words *grace* and *peace* in a dictionary and/or Bible dictionary.

Question 14. Notice that Paul and Timothy were joyful servants of God, while Paul and Silas were joyful prisoners for God. Paul could cheerfully sing and praise the Lord in any circumstance because he was laboring and suffering for the One he loved.

STUDY 2: PAUL'S PRAYER OF THANKSGIVING

Question 2. "The studied repetitions of the word *all*...is Paul's gentle reminder that there is no place for partisanship in the Christian community. Intercession is not a burden to be borne but an exercise of the soul to be performed with joy" (*The Wycliffe Bible Commentary,* p. 1321).

Question 6. In Philippians 1:7, Paul mentioned his imprisonment. Although Bible scholars are not in complete agreement on the location of this imprisonment, it seems most likely that Paul was under house arrest, probably chained to a Roman guard.

Question 7. Compare the "fruit of righteousness" with Galatians 5:22-25 in which Paul outlined the fruit of the Spirit and encouraged Christians to live "in step with the Spirit."

STUDY 3: IMPRISONMENT FOR CHRIST

Question 2. The Praetorian Guard or palace guard was an elite group of soldiers loyal to the Roman emperor. These *praetoriani* were in charge of the prisoners held in custody by Caesar.

Question 5. Here Paul seems to take an end-justifies-the-means approach. In reality, he was not supporting the motives of the preachers, but he gave glory to God for the furtherance of the gospel when repression could just as easily have happened. Shouldn't we view others with whom we disagree in the same light? If they draw attention to Christ rather than to themselves, we have no reason to contend with them.

Question 8. "Paul's own life had been so completely taken up with the person and program of his Lord that he could say, 'For me to live is Christ.' Christ was the sum total of his existence. 'To die is gain' because in the absence of life's limitations union with Christ will be completely realized" (*The Wycliffe Bible Commentary,* p. 1323). Paul also knew that he would benefit the kingdom of God by his life, and his willing death would bear witness and give confidence to both searching unbelievers and Christians.

Question 13. Various translations use other phrases for "your progress…in the faith" (Philippians 1:25), such as: "add to your progress," "help you progress," "for your furtherance," "help you grow," and "help you forward." Explore the meanings of each of these phrases.

STUDY 4: UNITY AND OBEDIENCE

Question 3. The fearlessness of the Christians served as a sign to the hostile groups in Philippi that their efforts to hurt the message of Christ were useless and would lead only to their own destruction. The Christians stood firm in their faith, proving to their enemies that the church could not be destroyed.

Question 4. "The privilege of suffering for Christ is the privilege of doing the kind of work for him that is important enough to merit the world's counterattack" (C. E. Simcox, *They Met at Philippi,* New York: Oxford University Press, 1958, p. 61).

Question 10. Many scholars believe that Philippians 2:6-11 was originally a hymn about Jesus. The consequence of Christ's suffering is that God exalted Jesus and "graciously conferred upon him the supreme name (either LORD, *kurios,* the OT name for God; or to be understood in the Hebrew sense of denoting rank and dignity)" (*The Wycliffe Bible Commentary,* p. 1325).

STUDY 5: THE CHRISTIAN LIFE IN ACTION

Question 3. Verses 12 and 13 of Philippians 2 may seem to contradict each other. While verse 12 urges us to work out our own salvation, as if we do it ourselves, verse 13 implies that God is the One who works for us. "Actually, however, these two verses may be brought into harmony by recognizing that because God is at work in believers, and God's grace is available, believers are able to achieve the purposes for which God has saved them" (Harold Lindsell, *Harper Study Bible,* Grand Rapids: Zondervan, 1965, p. 1759).

Question 8. Compare with Philippians 2:4. "There are ministers who preach, teach, pastor or write, not out of genuine concern for the furtherance of the gospel, but for their own interests, glory, prestige and selfish ambition. Rather than seeking to please the Lord Jesus, they seek instead to please people and gain their favor (vv. 20-21; 1:15; 2 Timothy 4:10, 16). Such ministers are not true servants of the Lord" (*The Full Life Study Bible,* Grand Rapids: Zondervan, 1990, p. 419).

Question 9. Epaphroditus, whose name means "charming," "is one of the most attractively heroic characters of the NT. He had been delegated to bring the gift of money (Philippians 4:18) and to serve Paul on behalf of the Philippians" (*The Wycliffe Bible Commentary,* p. 1326). He became deathly ill during his time of serving the Lord and his apostle—another example of "going all the way" for Christ.

STUDY 6: THE TRUE RIGHTEOUSNESS

Question 3. Compare Romans 2:28-29, which explains the difference between "outward" and "inward" circumcision.

Question 4. "Hebrew of the Hebrews" refers to the retaining of the Hebrew language. The Pharisees were a Jewish religious group especially strict in observing the fine points of Jewish Law.

Question 5. If you are not familiar with the story of Paul's conversion, read it in Acts 9:1-22.

Question 7. "The parallel clauses contrast works-righteousness, which is based on law, with faith-righteousness, which is given by God. Here is Paul's most concise statement of justification by faith" (*The Wycliffe Bible Commentary,* p. 1328).

STUDY 7: CITIZENS OF HEAVEN

Question 2. Keep in mind that Paul wasn't saying he had already achieved perfection (see Philippians 3:12); he was striving toward a heavenly goal rather than being sluggish in his

Christian journey. This is what he wanted the other Christians to imitate.

Question 5. "The normal attitude of the believer who is in this world but not of it, is to look for the coming of the Lord to celebrate His triumph over the powers of evil and perfect His work of redemption. The Christian rejoices in the prospect of living in the glory of Christ's presence, and of enjoying the bliss and delight of heaven's eternal home" (*Harper Study Bible,* p. 1760).

Question 8. "Stand firm" in Philippians 4:1 could be an introduction to Paul's appeal to the two women, Euodia and Syntyche. When Christians are in disagreement, it is impossible for them—and the church—to stand firm in the Lord. So Paul urged them to agree, not on a strictly human level, but because they were sisters in the Lord.

Question 9. The loyal yokefellow's identity is unknown. Some commentators cite Epaphroditus, some the bishop or minister of the Philippian church, others one of Paul's companions in prison. "It could also be someone named Syzygus, another way to understand the word for yokefellow" (*Life Application Bible,* Wheaton: Tyndale, 1991, p. 2153).

STUDY 8: REJOICE IN THE LORD ALWAYS

Question 3. Gentleness, or moderation, as some translate it, "indicates readiness to listen to reason, a yieldingness that does not retaliate. The motive for this 'sweet reasonableness' is the imminent return of Christ" (*The Wycliffe Bible Commentary,*

p. 1329). Note that some translations tie Philippians 4:5, "The Lord is near," to verses 6-8.

Question 5. "The one essential cure for worry is prayer, for the following reasons: (1) Through prayer we renew our trust in the Lord's faithfulness… (2) God's peace comes to guard our hearts and minds as a result of our communion with Christ Jesus… (3) God strengthens us to do all the things he desires of us… (4) We receive mercy, grace and help in time of need… (5) We are assured that in all things God works for our good" (*The Full Life Study Bible,* p. 421).

Question 7. C. E. Simcox calls this the "paragraph on mental health." These qualities that should dominate our thoughts will guard us from the evil—and because of evil, pain—which so easily infiltrates our minds, especially in today's society. Some commentators say Paul borrowed from the philosophers of his day in his composition of this passage.

Question 10. "In 1 Corinthians 9:11-18, Paul wrote that he didn't accept gifts from the Corinthian church because he didn't want to be accused of preaching only to get money. But Paul maintained that it was a church's responsibility to support God's ministers (1 Corinthians 9:14). He accepted the Philippians' gift because they gave it willingly and because he was in need" (*Life Application Bible,* p. 2154).

Question 12. "Those who belong to Caesar's household" (Philippians 4:22) refers to those in government service. It shows that already at this time there were Christians in government.

What Should We Study Next?

*J*f you enjoyed this Fisherman Bible Studyguide, you might want to explore our full line of Fisherman Resources and Bible Studyguides. The following books offer time-tested Fisherman inductive Bible studies for individuals or groups.

FISHERMAN RESOURCES

The Art of Spiritual Listening: Responding to God's Voice Amid the Noise of Life by Alice Fryling

Balm in Gilead by Dudley Delffs

The Essential Bible Guide by Whitney T. Kuniholm

Questions from the God Who Needs No Answers: What Is He Really Asking of You? by Carolyn and Craig Williford

Reckless Faith: Living Passionately As Imperfect Christians by Jo Kadlecek

Soul Strength: Spiritual Courage for the Battles of Life by Pam Lau

FISHERMAN BIBLE STUDYGUIDES

Topical Studies

Angels by Vinita Hampton Wright

Becoming Women of Purpose by Ruth Haley Barton

Building Your House on the Lord: A Firm Foundation for Family Life (Revised Edition) by Steve and Dee Brestin

Discipleship: The Growing Christian's Lifestyle by James and Martha Reapsome

Doing Justice, Showing Mercy: Christian Action in Today's World by Vinita Hampton Wright

Encouraging Others: Biblical Models for Caring by Lin Johnson

The End Times: Discovering What the Bible Says by E. Michael Rusten

Examining the Claims of Jesus by Dee Brestin

Friendship: Portraits in God's Family Album by Steve and Dee Brestin

The Fruit of the Spirit: Cultivating Christlike Character by Stuart Briscoe

Great Doctrines of the Bible by Stephen Board

Great Passages of the Bible by Carol Plueddemann

Great Prayers of the Bible by Carol Plueddemann

Growing Through Life's Challenges by James and Martha Reapsome

Guidance & God's Will by Tom and Joan Stark

Heart Renewal: Finding Spiritual Refreshment by Ruth Goring

Higher Ground: Steps Toward Christian Maturity by Steve and Dee Brestin

Images of Redemption: God's Unfolding Plan Through the Bible by Ruth E. Van Reken

Integrity: Character from the Inside Out by Ted W. Engstrom and Robert C. Larson

Lifestyle Priorities by John White

Marriage: Learning from Couples in Scripture by R. Paul and Gail Stevens

Miracles by Robbie Castleman

One Body, One Spirit: Building Relationships in the Church by Dale and Sandy Larsen

The Parables of Jesus by Gladys Hunt

Parenting with Purpose and Grace: Wisdom for Responding to Your Child's Deepest Needs by Alice Fryling

Prayer: Discovering What Scripture Says by Timothy Jones and Jill Zook-Jones

The Prophets: God's Truth Tellers by Vinita Hampton Wright

Proverbs and Parables: God's Wisdom for Living by Dee Brestin

Satisfying Work: Christian Living from Nine to Five by R. Paul Stevens and Gerry Schoberg

Senior Saints: Growing Older in God's Family by James and Martha Reapsome

The Sermon on the Mount: The God Who Understands Me by Gladys M. Hunt

Speaking Wisely: Exploring the Power of Words by Poppy Smith

Spiritual Disciplines: The Tasks of a Joyful Life by Larry Sibley

Spiritual Gifts by Karen Dockrey

Spiritual Hunger: Filling Your Deepest Longings by Jim and Carol Plueddemann

A Spiritual Legacy: Faith for the Next Generation by Chuck and Winnie Christensen

Spiritual Warfare: Disarming the Enemy Through the Power of God by A. Scott Moreau

The Ten Commandments: God's Rules for Living by Stuart Briscoe

Ultimate Hope for Changing Times by Dale and Sandy Larsen

When Faith Is All You Have: A Study of Hebrews 11 by Ruth E. Van Reken

Where Your Treasure Is: What the Bible Says About Money by James and Martha Reapsome

Who Is God? by David P. Seemuth

Who Is Jesus? In His Own Words by Ruth E. Van Reken

Who Is the Holy Spirit? by Barbara H. Knuckles and Ruth
E. Van Reken

Wisdom for Today's Woman: Insights from Esther by Poppy Smith

Witnesses to All the World: God's Heart for the Nations by Jim
and Carol Plueddemann

Women at Midlife: Embracing the Challenges by Jeanie Miley

Worship: Discovering What Scripture Says by Larry Sibley

Bible Book Studies

Genesis: Walking with God by Margaret Fromer and Sharrel
Keyes

Exodus: God Our Deliverer by Dale and Sandy Larsen

Ruth: Relationships That Bring Life by Ruth Haley Barton

Ezra and Nehemiah: A Time to Rebuild by James Reapsome
(For Esther, see Topical Studies, *Wisdom for Today's Woman*)

Job: Trusting Through Trials by Ron Klug

Psalms: A Guide to Prayer and Praise by Ron Klug

Proverbs: Wisdom That Works by Vinita Hampton Wright

Ecclesiastes: A Time for Everything by Stephen Board

Song of Songs: A Dialogue of Intimacy by James Reapsome

Jeremiah: The Man and His Message by James Reapsome

Jonah, Habakkuk, and Malachi: Living Responsibly by
Margaret Fromer and Sharrel Keyes

Matthew: People of the Kingdom by Larry Sibley

Mark: God in Action by Chuck and Winnie Christensen

Luke: Following Jesus by Sharrel Keyes

John: An Eyewitness Account of the Son of God by Whitney
T. Kuniholm

Acts 1–12: God Moves in the Early Church by Chuck and
Winnie Christensen

Acts 13–28 by Chuck and Winnie Christensen (formerly
  titled *Paul: Thirteenth Apostle*)
Romans: The Christian Story by James Reapsome
1 Corinthians: Problems and Solutions in a Growing Church by
  Charles and Ann Hummel
Strengthened to Serve: 2 Corinthians by Jim and Carol
  Plueddemann
Galatians, Titus, and Philemon: Freedom in Christ by Whitney
  Kuniholm
Ephesians: Living in God's Household by Robert Baylis
Philippians: God's Guide to Joy by Ron Klug
Colossians: Focus on Christ by Luci Shaw
Letters to the Thessalonians by Margaret Fromer and Sharrel
  Keyes
Letters to Timothy: Discipleship in Action by Margaret Fromer
  and Sharrel Keyes
Hebrews: Foundations for Faith by Gladys Hunt
James: Faith in Action by Chuck and Winnie Christensen
1 and 2 Peter, Jude: Called for a Purpose by Steve and Dee
  Brestin
1, 2, 3 John: How Should a Christian Live? by Dee Brestin
Revelation: The Lamb Who Is the Lion by Gladys Hunt

Bible Character Studies
Abraham: Model of Faith by James Reapsome
David: Man After God's Own Heart by Robbie Castleman
Elijah: Obedience in a Threatening World by Robbie
  Castleman
Great People of the Bible by Carol Plueddemann
King David: Trusting God for a Lifetime by Robbie Castleman

Men Like Us: Ordinary Men, Extraordinary God by Paul
   Heidebrecht and Ted Scheuermann
Moses: Encountering God by Greg Asimakoupoulos
Women Like Us: Wisdom for Today's Issues by Ruth Haley
   Barton
Women Who Achieved for God by Winnie Christensen
Women Who Believed God by Winnie Christensen

Kazam takes off her coat.

A bird is on her arm.

Kazam takes off her shoe.

A bird is on her foot.

Kazam waves her wand.

Birdseed!

HELPING YOUR BRAND-NEW READER

Here's how to make first-time reading easy and fun:

▶ Read the introduction at the beginning of the book aloud. Look through the pictures together so that your child can see what happens in the story before reading the words.

▶ Read one or two pages to your child, placing your finger under each word.

▶ Let your child touch the words and read the rest of the story. Give him or her time to figure out each new word.

▶ If your child gets stuck on a word, you might say, *"Try something. Look at the picture. What would make sense?"*

▶ If your child is still stuck, supply the right word. This will allow him or her to continue to read and enjoy the story. You might say, *"Could this word be 'ball'?"*

▶ Always praise your child. Praise what he or she reads correctly, and praise good tries too.

▶ Give your child lots of chances to read the story again and again. The more your child reads, the more confident he or she will become.

▶ Have fun!

BRAND
NEW
READERS™

There are some birds on Kazam. How can she make them fly away?

Includes advice to help you guide and support your brand-new reader.